𝔚ar 𝕮ook 𝔅ook

𝔉or 𝔄merican 𝔚omen

Suggestions for patriotic service in the home

Frederic J. Haskin

Alpha Editions

This edition published in 2020

ISBN : 9789354027314

Design and Setting By
Alpha Editions
email - alphaedis@gmail.com

The President's Call to the Women of the Nation

My Dear Mr. Hoover: It seems to me that the inauguration of that portion of the plan for Food Administration which contemplates a national mobilization of the great voluntary forces of the country which are ready to work toward saving food and eliminating waste admits of no further delay.

The approaching harvesting, the immediate necessity for wise use and saving, not only in food, but in all other expenditures, the many undirected and overlapping efforts being made toward this end, all press for national direction and inspiration.

The women of the nation are already earnestly seeking to do their part in this our greatest struggle for the maintenance of our national ideals, and in no direction can they so greatly assist as by enlisting in the service the Food Administration and cheerfully accepting its direction and advice. By so doing they will increase the surplus of food available for our own army and for export to the Allies. To provide adequate supplies for the coming year is of absolutely vital importance to the conduct of the war, and without a very conscientious elimination of waste and very strict economy in our food consumption, we cannot hope to fulfill this primary duty.

I trust, therefore, that the women of the country will not only respond to your appeal, and accept the pledge to the food administration which you are proposing, but that all men also who are engaged in the personal distribution of foods will cooperate with the same earnestness and in the same spirit. I give you full authority to undertake any steps necessary for the proper organization and stimulation of their efforts.

Cordially and sincerely yours,

Mr. Herbert C. Hoover,
Washington, D. C.
June 12, 1917.

Woodrow Wilson

War Service in the Home

THE PLEDGE

PLEDGE CARD FOR UNITED STATES FOOD
ADMINISTRATION

IF YOU HAVE ALREADY SIGNED, PASS THIS ON
TO A FRIEND

To the Food Administrator:

I am glad to join you in the service of food conservation for our nation and I hereby accept membership in the United States Food Administration, pledging myself to carry out the directions and advice of the Food Administrator in my home, in so far as my circumstances permit.

Name..

Street...

City.........................State...........

There are no fees or dues to be paid. The Food Administration wishes to have as members all of those actually handling food in the home.

Anyone may have the Home Card of Instruction, but only those signing pledges are entitled to Membership Window Card, which will be delivered upon receipt of the signed pledge.

1—262

The Food Conservation Campaign

The Food Conservation Campaign is a campaign to save food. The food that America saves will go far toward winning the war and saving civilization. There is a duty and a responsibility laid on every American household today. There must be a wise choice of food, no waste, and careful use. The women of America control nine-tenths of the consumption of food. The President of the United States calls upon patriotic women to do their duty, in an appeal which is printed on the first page of this book.

Millions of women have signed the pledge of cooperation. By so doing they have made a covenant with the government that, in managing their households from day to day, they will always remember the needs of the nation as told to them by the Food Administration.

The pledge is not a promise to so some particular thing, but an agreement to follow directions. Directions are issued to suit conditions that vary from day to day. In the spring, for example, when the stock of potatoes ran low, the directions said: Eat rice; but when the potato crop was harvested, the directions said: Eat potatoes, the rice is wanted for the Army.

The directions are carefully based on what is required by the whole nation, by the Army, and by the cause of honor and democracy for which we are making war. Each household must decide for itself how far it can follow the directions, according to the pledge, which reads, "in so far as my circumstances will permit." The country looks to each woman to do what she can. Just how much she will do is left to her individual conscience.

The directions are based on definite knowledge. Under Mr. Herbert Hoover in the Food Administration, and under Dr. R. L. Wilbur in the Food Conservation Division, all that can be known of the country's supply of different foods, of their food values and how they can be substituted, one for another, is carefully compiled and studied. How much grain we can spare is known, and how much our Allies need. It is known how much barley and rye they can work into their war bread, and how much wheat we must send them. The American woman who pledges her cooperation in the Food Conservation Campaign can be sure that the directions she receives have been drawn up by men and women who know, and who will not ask her for any saving which can possibly deprive her family of any necessary foodstuffs.

When the Food Administration proposes that everyone eat one more potato instead of that other slice of bread, it means that so many million bushels of wheat can be sent to the armies of our Allies fighting in Europe. We eat the potatoes and send the wheat, instead of eating the wheat and sending the potatoes, because a ship will carry three times as much food in the form of wheat.

When the Food Administration again recommends corn muffins instead of toast, it means that by going on a partial war diet we can spare so many more million bushels of wheat for our Allies, who are already eating war bread. We send wheat instead of corn, because wheat bread can be made into baker's loaves, and will keep, while corn-bread cannot. When Americans are urged to eat more fish and poultry instead of meat, or to save a third of an ounce of butter a day, it means that the Food Administration knows—and knows definitely—in ounces and pounds—what America must do to save America's Allies from starving.

Food—the necessary foodstuffs—must be saved in America or the Allies will be weakened, and the cause may be lost. At the very least, victory will be so much more dearly bought in American blood and American lives. Wheat and red meat and fats must be spared from America's stores, or the soldiers and workers of the Allies will want, and the little children will pine away. The Government cannot save food; it must be done by the people, by each woman in her own home. Through making and keeping the volunteer pledge the women—and the men—of this land will see that America does her part to prevent distress at home, to serve the cause of humanity, to see that democracy does not perish from the earth—to put the Golden Rule above the Iron Law.

HOME CARD

(1918)

United States Food Administration

WHAT YOU CAN DO TO HELP WIN THIS WAR

OUR PROBLEM is to feed the Allies and our own soldiers abroad by sending them as much food as we can of the most concentrated nutritive value in the least shipping space. These foods are wheat, beef, pork, butter and sugar.

OUR SOLUTION is to eat less of these and as little of all foods as will support health and strength. These foods are wheat, beef, pork, butter and sugar.

The Food Administration asks every loyal American to help win the war by maintaining rigidly, **AS A MINIMUM OF SAVING,** the following program:

Have **TWO WHEATLESS DAYS** (Monday and Wednesday) in every week, and **ONE WHEATLESS MEAL** in every day.

> **EXPLANATION**—On "Wheatless" days and in "Wheatless" meals of other days use no bread, crackers, pastry, breakfast food or other cereal food containing wheat or wheat flour in any form except the small amount that may be needed for thickening soups or gravies, or for a binder in corn bread and other cereal breads. If you buy your bread do not buy any containing more than 70 per cent of wheat flour.

Have **ONE MEATLESS DAY** (Tuesday) in every week and **ONE MEATLESS MEAL** in every day. Have **TWO PORKLESS DAYS** (Tuesday and Saturday) in every week.

EXPLANATION—"Meatless" means without any beef, pork or mutton, fresh or preserved. On other days use mutton in preference to beef. "Porkless" means without pork, bacon, ham, lard or pork products, fresh or preserved. As a nation we eat and waste nearly twice as much meat as we need.

Make every day a **FAT-SAVING DAY** (butter, lard, lard-substitutes, cottonseed oil, etc.).

EXPLANATION—Fry less. You can bake, broil, boil or stew foods instead. Save your meat drippings if you are not doing so now and use them in cooking instead of butter. Butter has food values vital to children; therefore, give it to them, but use as little as possible for yourself. Use vegetable oils instead of butter or lard in cooking. Waste no soap; it is made from fat. We use and waste two and a half times more fat than we need.

Make every day a **SUGAR-SAVING DAY.**

EXPLANATION—Use less sugar in the household. Less candy and sweet drinks should be used in war time. As a nation we have used twice as much sugar as we need.

Use **VEGETABLES AND FRUITS** abundantly.

EXPLANATION—Vegetables and fruits are healthful and plentiful, and, at the same time, partly take the place of other foods which we should save. Raise vegetables and fruits for home use.

Use **MILK** wisely.

EXPLANATION—Use all of the milk; waste no part of it. The children must have whole milk. Use sour milk in cooking and as cottage cheese.

HOARDING FOOD. Any one buying and holding a larger supply of food now than in peace time, except foods canned, dried or preserved in the home, is helping to defeat the Food Administration in its attempt to secure a just distribution of food and the establishment of fair prices. The food hoarder is working against the common good and even against the very safety of the country. Hoarding food in households is both selfish and unnecessary, as the Government is protecting the food supply of its people.

Loyalty in little things is the foundation of the national strength. **DISLOYALTY IN LITTLE THINGS GIVES AID TO THE ENEMY. KEEP THE PLEDGE.**

Do not limit the food of growing children.

Eat sufficient food to maintain health; the nation needs strong people.

Cooperate with your local and federal food administrators. Accept their advice.

Preach and practice the "gospel of the clean plate."

Housekeepers should cooperate with stores to cut down deliveries.

Use local supplies and save railroad transportation.

Report to the nearest food administration officer the name and address of any person discouraging the production or saving of food.

Why We Must Save Food

To the Members of the United States Food Administration:

The men of the Allied Nations are fighting; they are not on the farms. Even the men of the European neutral countries are under arms. The fields of both Allies and neutrals lack man-power, fertilizer and machinery. Hence, the production of food by these countries has steadily lessened ever since the beginning of the war, while, at the same time, the shortage of shipping has grown more and more serious, with the consequent steady increase of difficulties in bringing food from the far-away markets of India, Australia and the Argentine.

The situation has become critical. There is simply not enough food in Europe, yet the soldiers of the Allies must be maintained in full strength; their wives and children at home must not face famine; the friendly neutrals must not be starved; and, finally, our own army in France must never lack a needed ounce of food.

There is just one way in which all these requirements can be met. North America must furnish the food. And it must furnish it from its savings because it has already sent its normal surplus.

We do not need to starve our own people. We have plenty for ourselves, and it is the firm policy of the Food Administration to retain for our people, by its control of exports, a sufficient supply of every essential foodstuff. We want nobody in our country to eat less than is necessary for good health and full strength, for America needs the full productive power of all its people. Much of the needed saving can be effected by substituting one kind of food for another in our diet. But the time has come to put aside all selfishness and disloyalty. The time has come for sacrifice.

The Allies ask us to meet only their absolutely imperative needs. They are restricting the consumption of their own people to the minimum necessary for health and strength. They are controlling their food by drastic government regulation. There is even actual privation among their women and children; there is starvation in Belgium.

The Allies need wheat and meat and fats and sugar. They must have more of all of these than we have been sending, more than we shall be able to send unless we restrict our own consumption. As a nation, we are today eating and wasting much more food than we need.

The whole great problem of winning the war rests primarily on one thing: the loyalty and sacrifice of the American people in the matter of food. It is not a government responsibility; it is the responsibility of each individual. Each pound of food saved by each American citizen is a pound given to the support of our army, the Allies and the friendly neutrals. Each pound wasted or eaten unnecessarily is a pound withheld from them. It is absolutely a personal obligation on the part of each of us to some one in Europe whom we are bound to help.

If we are selfish or even careless, we are disloyal, we are the enemy at home. Now is the hour of our testing. Let us make it the hour of our victory; victory over ourselves; victory over the Enemy of Freedom.

HERBERT HOOVER,
United States Food Administrator.

Service Suggestions

Join the Service Army

Everybody must pull together. The consumer must help to see to it that the farmer gets reasonable prices for his products. The farmer must help the government to protect the consumer from the extortion of unscrupulous and disloyal food speculators.

Go Back to the Simple Life

Be contented with simple food, simple pleasures, simple clothes. Work hard, pray hard, play hard. Work, eat, recreate, and sleep. Do it all courageously. We have a victory to win.

Keep Fit

It is the duty of every citizen to keep himself in good health. This means proper exercise and sleep. It also means careful attention to food. Eat the right things, the proper combinations, and the right amount. Follow these principles laid down by the United States Food Administration.

Buy less; cook no more than necessary; serve smaller portions.

Use local and seasonable supplies.

Patronize your local producers and lessen the need of transportation.

Preach and practice the "gospel of the clean plate."

We do not ask the American people to starve themselves. Eat plenty, but wisely, and without waste.

Do not limit the plain food of growing children.

Do not eat between meals.

Watch out for the waste in the community.

Don't Waste Food by Serving too Much

Cook just enough for your family. Do not imagine you are going to have unexpected guests. The chances are that you will only waste good food. Serve smaller portions, so that none will be left upon the plates.

Don't Try Dangerous Experiments

Careless cooking must go. We must not conduct wasteful experiments. Let the departments at Washington and at your State universities do the experimenting for you.

Store your Root Vegetables Carefully for Winter Use

We have an abundance of vegetables. Root vegetables will keep if carefully stored. Can and dry the others. The widespread use of vegetables will insure the health of our people.

Don't let Perishable Foods Perish in Your House

Buy only what you need. See that it is put away clean and kept in a cool place.

Plan Meals and do Your Ordering Ahead of Time

This helps your butcher, your baker and your groceryman to have the right amount of material on hand. You avoid waste at home.

Save Fuel

Never leave gas burning when you are not using it. Matches cost less than gas. If you use coal or wood plan to use the oven when a hot fire must be built for other reasons. On baking day roast meat, bake potatoes or apples or plan a casserole dish.

Don't try to make water reach a higher temperature than boiling. A high flame after the water boils wastes gas. Air out the oven before starting the fire. It will heat much more quickly.

Make the New Foods Appetizing and Attractive

By means of garnishes, sauces and judicious seasoning and flavoring the housewife can make her family vote themselves in favor of the new foods. Conversion in this case is patriotism.

Heat only the Rooms You Use this Winter

The fewer fires you can burn the better. Be especially careful in the use of coal. Burn wood if you can get it. Coal must be brought by the railroads and they are needed for war purposes.

Keep in Touch with Your Local Council of Defense and with the United States Food Administration

They have much to tell you. Have your name put on the mailing lists. Get the new recipes, cards and bulletins. Get speakers from your State Council to come and tell you about the work they are doing and the work you can do.

Good Food Is Wasted

If it gets into the garbage pail.
If allowed to spoil in the home.
If ruined by careless cooking.
If carelessly pared and trimmed.
If too much is served at a meal.
Make saving, rather than spending, your social standard.

Let Us Remember

Let us remember that every flag that flies opposite the German one is by proxy the American flag, and that the armies fighting in our defense under these flags can not be maintained through this winter unless there is food enough for them and for their women and children at home. There can only be food enough if America provides it. And America can only provide it by the personal service and patriotic cooperation of all of us.

The Soldiers Need	The Folks at Home Can Use	
Wheat	Corn	
	Oats	
	Barley	
	Rye	
Butter	Cottonseed Oil	
Lard	Peanut Oil	For cooking
	Corn Oil	
	Drippings	
Sugar	Molasses	
	Honey	
	Syrups	
Beef	Chicken	
Ham	Nuts	
Mutton	Eggs	
	Cottage Cheese	
	Fish	

Household War Orders

THE FOOD CONSERVATION CAMPAIGN IN TERMS OF THE KITCHEN AND PANTRY

Let This Be Your Saving Schedule

1 ounce of sugar per person per day.
$\frac{1}{3}$ ounce of fat per person per day.
2 ounces of wheat flour per person per day.

1 ounce of sugar measures 2 level tablespoons.
$\frac{1}{3}$ ounce of butter measures 2 level teaspoons.
2 ounces of flour measures $\frac{1}{4}$ cup.

Study This Problem in Arithmetic

100,000,000 persons in the United States.

100,000,000 x 1 ounce of sugar = 100,000,000 ounces of sugar.

100,000,000 x $\frac{1}{3}$ ounce of fat = 33,333,333 ounces of fat.

100,000,000 x 2 ounces of wheat flour = 200,000,000 ounces of wheat flour.

100,000,000 ounces x 365 (days in one year) = 2,281,250,000 pounds of sugar.

33,333,333 ounces x 365 (days in one year) = 760,416,545 pounds of fat.

200,000,000 ounces x 365 (days in one year) = 73,000,000,000 pounds of wheat flour.

This is the amount of sugar, fat and wheat flour that we can save in one year.

Study Your Menus

Ask yourself the following questions about your menus:

I. Are you using as much as possible of products raised near your home or are you making the railroads haul your food when they ought to be hauling supplies for the Army?

II. Are you working to save 25 per cent of the wheat—the wheat that will win the war?

III. Have you used beef, mutton or pork when you might have substituted such muscle-building foods as cheese or beans?

IV. Does your menu provide for a one-third reduction in sugar? (Americans have been urgently asked to save this amount for our Allies, the French.)

V. Does your menu provide plenty of whole milk for the children?

Food Elements

Eat Something from Each of These Five Groups Every Day

Group I. Foods for Mineral Matter, acids and body regulators.
Group II. Protein Foods.
Group III. Starchy Foods.
Group IV. Foods for Sugar.
Group V. Foods for Fat.

GROUP I

Eat Vegetables and Fruits for Mineral Matter, Acids and Body Regulators. Eat Freely of all These

APPLES	GREEN OR	PEARS
APRICOTS	CANNED CORN	GREEN OR
ASPARAGUS	CUCUMBERS	CANNED PEAS
BANANAS	GRAPES	PINEAPPLE
LIMA BEANS	LEMONS	RHUBARB
BEETS	LETTUCE	SPINACH
BLACKBERRIES	MUSKMELON	SQUASH
CABBAGE	ONIONS	STRAWBERRIES
CARROTS	ORANGES	STRING BEANS
CAULIFLOWER	PARSNIPS	TOMATOES
CELERY	PEACHES	TURNIPS

GROUP II

Eat These Foods for Protein. Eat Sparingly of Those Written with the Small Type, Eat Freely of all Others

BEANS	AMERICAN CHEESE	GAME	OYSTERS
SOY	COTTAGE CHEESE	LAMB	PEANUTS
LIMA	EGGS	SKIM MILK	PEAS
NAVY	FISH	Mutton	Pork
Beef	FOWL	NUTS	RABBITS
			Veal

GROUP III

Eat These Foods for Starches. Eat Sparingly of Those in Small Type but Freely of all the Others

BARLEY	Graham Crackers	WHITE POTATOES
White Bread	Cream of Wheat	SWEET POTATOES
Cake	Farina	RICE
GREEN OR	Wheat Flour	RYE
CANNED CORN	HOMINY	TAPIOCA
CORNFLAKES	Macaroni	Wheat Breakfast
CORN MEAL	OATMEAL	Foods
Soda Crackers	ROLLED OATS	

GROUP IV

Eat These Foods for Sugar.   Eat Sparingly of the One in Small Type.   Eat Freely of the Others

DRIED APPLES	HONEY	PRUNES
CANE SYRUPS	MAPLE SYRUP	RAISINS
CORN SYRUP	MOLASSES	SORGHUM
DATES	DRIED PEACHES	Sugar

GROUP V

Eat These Foods for Fat.   Eat Sparingly of Those in Small Type; Be Careful of all Fats.

Bacon	CORN OIL	OLIVE OIL
Butter	Cream	PEANUT BUTTER
CHOCOLATE	Lard	PEANUT OIL
COCOA	OLEOMARGARINE	Salt Pork

Try the Following Meat Saving Schedule

Day	Protein	Foods	Served
Sunday............	Eggs (Poached)	Chicken (Baked)	Milk (Sherbert)
Monday...........	Beans (Baked)	Leftover Chicken (Chicken Salad) or Fish (Broiled)	Milk
Tuesday...........	Eggs (Omelet)	Fish (Creamed)	Milk (Junket)
Wednesday........	Cottage Cheese	Peas (Purée)	Milk
Thursday..........	Macaroni and Cheese	Peanuts (Loaf)	Milk
Friday............	Fish (Baked)	American Cheese (Cheese Fondue)	Milk
Saturday..........	Beans (Loaf)	Eggs and Milk (Custard)	Milk

Plan Well-Selected Meals

The following gives a day's ample nourishment:

BREAKFAST
Group   I.   Prunes
Group   II.   Eggs—Milk
Group III.   Graham Muffins—Oatmeal or Baked Potato
Group   IV.   Jam
Group   V.   Butter

LUNCH OR SUPPER
Group   I.   Vegetables in Salad
Group   II.   Milk to Drink
Group III.   Corn Meal Muffins
Group   IV.   Honey in Honey Cakes
Group   V.   Butter—Salad Dressing

DINNER
Group   I.   Spinach—Apple in Pudding
Group   II.   Fish—Egg and Milk in Pudding
Group III.   Potatoes—Rye Bread
Group   IV.   Sugar in Coffee and in Pudding
Group   V.   Butter—Cream in Coffee

Save the Wheat

SAVE TWO OUNCES OF WHEAT FLOUR FOR EVERY PERSON IN YOUR FAMILY EVERY DAY

The three slices of white bread omitted means one-fourth cup (2 ounces) of flour saved. Eat more potatoes, and rice. Eat corn bread instead of wheat bread.

Try the New War Breads where Other Materials Have been Substituted for Part of the Wheat

WAR BREADS

Barley Yeast Bread

1 cup milk and water or water
1 tablespoon sugar (if desired)
1 tablespoon fat (if desired)
1 teaspoon salt
1^1/6 cups barley flour
2$\frac{1}{3}$ cups wheat flour
$\frac{1}{2}$ cake compressed yeast

Rice Yeast Bread

1$\frac{1}{2}$ cup milk and water or water
4 tablespoons sugar (if desired)
4 tablespoons fat (if desired)
1$\frac{1}{2}$ teaspoons salt
7 cups boiled rice
8 cups flour
$\frac{1}{2}$ cake compressed yeast
$\frac{1}{4}$ cup warm water

Corn Meal Yeast Bread

1$\frac{1}{4}$ cups milk and water or water
2 tablespoons sugar (if desired)
1 tablespoon fat (if desired)
2 teaspoons salt
$\frac{2}{3}$ cup corn meal
2$\frac{1}{3}$ cups flour
$\frac{1}{2}$ cake compressed yeast
$\frac{1}{4}$ cup warm water

Add sugar, fat and salt to liquid and bring to boiling point. Add corn meal slowly, stirring constantly until all is added. Remove from fire, cool mixture, and add compressed yeast softened in $\frac{1}{4}$ cup warm water. Add 2$\frac{1}{3}$ cups flour and knead. Let rise until about double its bulk, knead again, and put in pan. When light, bake in moderate oven for at least an hour.

Save Wheat by Applying the "Fifty-Fifty" Rule

"Fifty-Fifty" Biscuits

2 cups corn meal, ground soy beans or finely ground peanuts, rice, flour or other substitute.
2 cups white flour
4 teaspoons baking powder
2 teaspoons salt
4 tablespoons shortening (if desired)
Liquid sufficient to mix to proper consistency (1–1½ cups)

"Fifty-Fifty" Rye Yeast Bread

1 cup milk and water, or water
1 tablespoon fat (if desired)
2 tablespoons sugar (if desired)
1 teaspoon salt
2¼ cups rye flour
2¼ cups wheat flour
½ cake compressed yeast
2 tablespoons water

"Fifty-Fifty" Corn Meal Griddle Cakes

1 cup sour milk
¾ cup flour
¾ cup corn meal
½ teaspoon soda
1 teaspoon baking powder
½ teaspoon salt
1 egg

Use Barley

Ask your local dealer to get barley meal and barley flour for you.

Barley Scones

1 cup whole wheat flour
1 cup barley meal
¼ teaspoon salt
2 teaspoons baking powder
2 tablespoons fat
¾ cup sour milk
⅓ teaspoon soda

Sift flour, barley meal, salt, baking powder and soda together and work in fat with tips of fingers or two knives. Combine flour mixture and sour milk to form a soft dough. Turn out on a well-floured board, knead slightly, roll to one-half inch thickness; cut in diamond shapes and bake in a hot oven.

Barley Muffins

1 cup whole wheat flour	1 egg
1 cup barley meal	1¼ cups sour milk
¼ teaspoon salt	½ teaspoon soda
2 teaspoons baking powder	2 tablespoons fat

Sift flour, barley meal, salt, baking powder and soda. Combine flour mixture and sour milk. Add beaten egg and melted fat. Bake in muffin pans in moderate oven.

Cut Your Bread at the Table

Follow the old fashion. Cut each slice of bread at the table as it is needed. This custom will help to save our wheat supply.

Use Every Crumb of Stale Bread

Use stale bread for bread puddings, for chicken or turkey dressings, for soups, for part of the flour in bread, cakes, griddle cakes and biscuits. Dry it thoroughly and make crumbs to use on casserole dishes, for croquettes and meat balls, for stuffings for peppers and whole canned tomatoes.

Cut the Bread Thin

Do not serve new bread. It is unsatisfying and one eats more than is necessary. Cut the slices thin. You are not being deprived of food. Simply eat more of other things than bread.

Sponge Cake without Wheat

4 eggs	1 tablespoon lemon juice
1 cup sugar	⅛ teaspoon salt
1 cup barley flour	

Separate the whites and yolks of eggs, beat yolks, add lemon juice and sugar, then flour. Fold in well-beaten whites of eggs and bake in slow oven.

Substitutes for a Loaf of Bread

6 to 7 Sweet Potatoes
13 Irish Potatoes
1³/₅ cups Rice
4 cups Rolled Oats
2 cups Hominy
8 Corn Meal Muffins
2¹/₅ cups Corn Meal Mush (uncooked)
14 Corn Meal Griddle Cakes
1 cup Indian Pudding
   (½ cup Corn Meal, 4 cups Milk)
9 Oatmeal Cookies (3 inches in diameter)
18 Peanut Cookies (2 inches in diameter)

Each of these amounts will give the same amount of energy as a loaf of bread.

Use Corn Starch or Rice Flour for Thickening

Use these instead of wheat flour in making white sauce, brown sauce, gravy, pudding sauce, puddings.

Save Meat

One or Two Meatless Days Every Week Will Help Win the War

Serve bean loaf, cheese dishes, omelets, and milk. Serve fish, rabbits, and poultry raised at home. These foods take the place of meat. Use them freely.

SUBSTITUTE FOR 2 POUNDS OF SIRLOIN STEAK

1⅔ pounds chicken   5 quarts milk
2 pounds fresh salmon   23 eggs
2²/₉ pounds halibut

These amounts give as much body-building food as do 2 pounds of sirloin steak.

GIVE COTTAGE CHEESE A FAIR TRIAL

Cottage cheese, the curd of sour milk, is one of the most important meat substitutes. It supplies more protein per pound than most meats and is considerably cheaper. Make cottage cheese sandwiches. Serve cottage cheese balls with salads. Combine it with chopped pimento and peppers and serve with salad dressing.

USE THE SKIM MILK

Use it liberally for cream soups, creamed and scalloped dishes, desserts, cottage cheese and chowders.

Use Vegetables

Eat all the Potatoes You Want

Eat them three times a day. Serve them baked, broiled, riced, mashed, warmed over, creamed, with fish, and in soups. Use them in making pancakes, bread, rolls and biscuits. Use them to take the place of part of the wheat bread. Never waste them. Their starch and mineral content is valuable.

Learn to Use Beans

Soy Beans   Navy Beans   Lima Beans

Make bean soup, baked beans, succotash, bean loaf or roast, bean pureés.

Baked Soy Beans

1½ cups yellow soy beans
½ cup navy beans
⅓ cup sugar
¼ teaspoonful mustard
1 small onion
¼ pound salt pork

Soak beans 12 hours, put in baking dish in which the salt pork, onion, sugar and mustard have been placed. Cover with cold water and cook in a slow oven at least 12 hours.

Lima Bean Roast

1 pt. dried Lima beans
½ pt. peanuts
½ pt. stale bread crumbs
1 teaspoonful onion juice
1 teaspoonful salt
Pepper

Soak beans 12 hours. Cover with water and boil until tender. Press through colander. Put peanuts through meat grinder. Mix with bean pulp.

Put the Peanut on Your Table

Peanuts are a valuable food. They contain as much protein as beans. They are comparatively cheap. Learn to use them.

Peanut Soup

1½ pints peanuts
3 quarts water
1 bay leaf
½ cup celery
1 slice onion
1 quart milk

Peanut Loaf

1 cup roasted peanuts
2 cups bread crumbs
¼ cup melted fat
½ teaspoonful onion juice
1 egg
½ teaspoonful salt
¼ teaspoonful pepper
Milk

Soak peanuts overnight in 2 quarts of water; in the morning, drain, add remaining water, bay leaf, celery and onion; boil this slowly 4 or 5 hours, stirring frequently to prevent burning, or boil 15 minutes and place in fireless cooker over night. Rub through sieve and return to fire. When again hot add the milk and let soup boil up; then season and serve.

To the peanuts, bread crumbs melted fat, beaten egg, cnion juice, salt and pepper, add enough milk to make a moist loaf. Add more seasoning if desired. Put into a greased tin or mold, bake for one hour in a moderate oven, covering the first half of the time. Turn out on a hot dish, sprinkle with chopped peanuts and serve with brown sauce.

Twenty Ways of Using Corn

See if this list does not suggest possibilities to you.

Corn Meal	Hominy	Green, Dried or Canned Corn
Pone	Breakfast Food	Succotash
Mush	Griddle Cakes	Corn Oysters
Cake	Muffins	Corn Fritters
Bread	Soup	Soup
Muffins	Slices, Browned with	Chowder
Yeast Bread	Meat Pudding	Escalloped Corn
Indian Pudding	Pudding	
Brown Bread		

Save Water in Which Vegetables Were Boiled

Make cream soups by using this water to thin a white sauce, and season as desired. Vegetables and leaves which cannot be used for any other purpose can "do their bit" in the soup kettle.

Boil Potatoes in Their Jackets

Much valuable material lies close to the skin of a potato. Thick parings cheat the consumer.

Losses in Cooking

Potatoes, pared before boiling, lose into the water in which they are cooked about one-fifth of the iron they contain; peas and beans lose from one-third to two-fifths, and spinach one-half of the total amount present. This variation is because of the relative amount of surface exposed in the different vegetables.

The amount of iron in our foods is small. Its importance to the body is great. We should conserve it to the greatest possible extent. To do this we should either steam our vegetables or use the water in which they are cooked. If potatoes are boiled and the water thrown away, they should be boiled "in their jackets."

Peel potatoes after cooking.

Preserve Your Own Eggs

1. Coat them with water glass. Use 9 parts water to 1 part water glass which can be obtained at the drug store.

2. Pack them in sawdust or small end down. Use wooden box. Keep them cool.

Learn to Test Your Eggs

"Candle" your eggs. Use a box with a hole cut in one side. Slip the box over an electric bulb or a lamp. Darken the room. Hold the egg with large end up before the opening in the box. Good eggs look clear and firm. The air cell is not larger than a dime. A large air cell and dark, freely moving yolk show that the egg is stale. Shell contents which appear black or very dark indicate a bad egg.

Use the Left-Overs

MEAT

Use left-over meat in meat pies, meat salads, meat balls, meat dumplings, hash, meat loaf, casserole dishes, creamed meat, meat and vegetable stews, soups or in omelets.

POTATO

Combine potato with meat as above.   Or make potato soufflés, soups potato balls, potato pancakes, potato bread, potato cake, creamed potatoes, fish balls.

BREAD

Use for bread puddings, chicken or turkey dressing, soups, part of the flour in bread, cakes, griddle cakes and biscuits.   Dry it thoroughly and make crumbs to use on scalloped dishes for stuffing for peppers and whole canned tomatoes.

CAKE

Use left-over cake for puddings.

VEGETABLES

Use left-over vegetables for salads, soups, chowders, in meat loaves, in casserole dishes or as a garnish for a roast and other dishes or as creamed vegetables.

MILK

Use all the milk—whether whole or skimmed.   Make soups, white sauces, gravys, sherbets, ice cream, custards, junket, gelatin sponges, and Bavarian creams.   Make cottage cheese and chowders.   Use it in scalloped dishes.   Buttermilk and sour milk with soda make excellent quick breads, pancakes and cakes.   Milk for which there is no other use should go to feed chickens.

CHEESE SCRAPS

Grate hard cheese and use it for macaroni dishes, sauces and sandwiches.   Keep fresh cheese wrapped in a cloth dipped in vinegar and wrung dry.

Skimmed Milk Recipes
RICE PUDDING

1 quart skimmed milk	½ teaspoonful salt
⅓ cup rice	⅓ cup sugar

Wash rice, mix ingredients, and pour into greased pudding dish; bake three hours in very slow oven, stirring three times during the first hour of baking to prevent rice from settling.

Variations.—One cup raisins may be added to make Rice and Raisin Pudding. Two tablespoonfuls sugar may be caramelized, dissolved in hot water, and added to the milk to make Caramel Rice Pudding.

The flavor may be changed and cost reduced by substituting ½ cup molasses and ½ teaspoon cinnamon for the sugar.

CORNSTARCH PUDDING

1 quart skimmed milk, scalded	¼ teaspoon salt
½ cup cold skimmed milk	¼ cup sugar
½ cup cornstarch	1 teaspoon vanilla.

Mix cornstarch, sugar, salt and cold skimmed milk. Add to scalded skimmed milk, stirring constantly until mixture thickens, afterward occasionally; cook until raw starch taste disappears. Turn into a wet mold and cool. Unmold and serve.

Variations.—Melt two squares of chocolate and add to the scalded skimmed milk.

Caramelize 3 tablespoons sugar, dissolve in hot water to make a syrup and add to the scalded, skimmed milk.

INDIAN PUDDING

5 cups scalded skimmed milk	1 teaspoon salt
⅓ cup Indian meal	1 teaspoon ginger
½ cup molasses	

Pour skimmed milk slowly on meal, cook in double boiler twenty minutes, add molasses, salt, and ginger; pour into greased pudding-dish and bake two hours in slow oven. Ginger may be omitted.

Variations.—One teaspoonful oleomargarine may be added to improve the flavor. Any ground cereal may replace the cornmeal to vary the flavor.

IVORY JELLY

1½ tablespoonfuls granulated gelatin	¼ cup sugar
½ cup cold skimmed milk	¼ teaspoon salt
2½ cups scalded skimmed milk	¾ teaspoon cinnamon

Soak gelatin in cold skimmed milk and dissolve in scalded skimmed milk. Add sugar, salt, and cinnamon. Strain into mold and chill.

Save Sugar

HOW WE WASTE SUGAR

In the bottom of the coffee cup.
Too much on cereal breakfast foods.
More than is necessary in breads and biscuits.
By careless cooking when something is spoiled.
By using a heavier (denser) syrup than is necessary in canning fruits.

Use Syrups and Honey in Place of Sugar in Cooking

BAKED HONEY CUSTARD

2 cups milk
3 eggs
¼ cup honey
⅛ teaspoon powdered cinnamon
¼ teaspoon salt

Scald milk, beat eggs slightly. Add honey, milk, cinnamon and salt. Bake in custard cups set in a pan of water.

DATE PUDDING

3 tablespoons fat
1 cup molasses
½ cup sweet milk
1½ cups flour
¼ teaspoon salt
¼ teaspoon nutmeg
¼ teaspoon allspice
¼ teaspoon cloves
½ pound dates

Stone and chop the dates, melt the fat, add to it the molasses and milk. Mix and sift dry ingredients and add to liquid. Add dates last of all. Steam 1½ hours.

RAISIN PIE

2 cups raisins
½ cup currants
2 cups water
1 cup honey
2 well-beaten eggs

Juice of 1 orange
Juice of 1 lemon
½ rind, grated, of orange or lemon
1 tablespoon butter substitute
Dried bread crumbs to thicken

Stew raisins and currants in water until tender. Add other ingredients in order mentioned. Bake in one crust with strips of pastry across the top.

Eat Natural Sweets in Place of Candy

Eat dates and figs and other sweet fruits. Eat maple sugar and honey, where you can get it, instead of candy.

Spread Bread with Jam Instead of Butter

Eating a slice of corn-bread spread with jam or fruit saves both wheat and butter. Use maple syrup, honey, and corn, sorghum and cane syrups, without butter, on pancakes and waffles.

Serve Simple Refreshments at Parties

Give your guests apples and other fruit, salted popcorn without butter, and candy made without sugar.

Candy Without Sugar

2 cups raisins
1 cup nuts
¼ cup honey

Grind nuts and raisins in food chopper. Mix with honey. Pack under a weight for 24 hours. Cut into bars.

Popcorn Has Power

Popcorn is very valuable as a food. Give the children popcorn balls made with honey or corn syrup. The children will be happy and satisfied, and you will be helping your country by saving on other sweets.

Save Fats

Keep a "Butter-Cup"

Save the small amounts of butter left on plates. Scrape it into a cup kept for that purpose. Use it for "special" cooking.

Use Other Fats in Place of Butter and Lard

Chicken fat makes good pastry. Solidified vegetable oils are valuable. Oleomargarine may often be used. Drippings and bacon fat are worth their weight in gold. Use these in any cooking.

Learn to Use the Vegetable Oils

Use corn oil, cottonseed oil, peanut oil and olive oil for cooking and frying as well as in salad dressings.

Make Soap of Fat Unfit for Cooking

Use lye made by letting water drip slowly through wood ashes, or buy lye in cans. Use porcelain or enamel dish. Dissolve 1 can lye in 1 quart cold water. Melt 5 pounds fat in separate dish. Strain through 2 thicknesses cheese cloth. Cool till lukewarm. Add dissolved cooled lye. Stir until mixture is like porridge. Pour quickly into shallow pasteboard boxes or dripping pan. When cool, crease into cakes. Cut when nearly cold.

Why not have a community soap making club?

Meat Trimmings Are Valuable

If you buy meat get the trimmings, try out the fat and use it in cooking.

Don't Waste Any Soap

Save pieces of soap too small to handle, melt them in a little water over a slow fire, use for washing dishes or boiling clothes.